BE BRAVE, BE BRAVE, BE BRAVE

by F. Anthony Falcon
illustrations by Trisha Mason

Brooklyn, NY

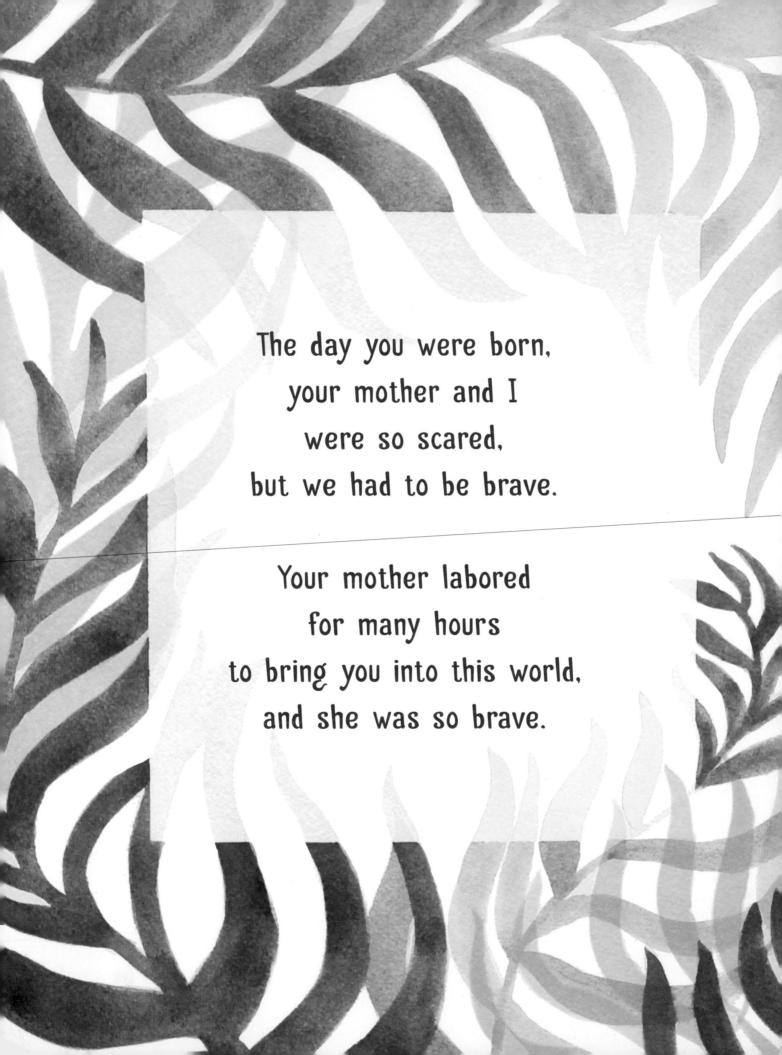

The day you were born,
your mother and I
were so scared,
but we had to be brave.

Your mother labored
for many hours
to bring you into this world,
and she was so brave.

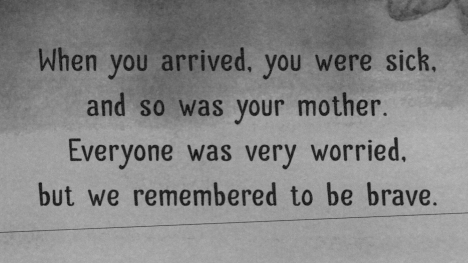

When you arrived, you were sick,
and so was your mother.
Everyone was very worried,
but we remembered to be brave.

We wanted to pay tribute
to my Native American ancestry,
so we named you Lakota,
after the Lakota Sioux people,
who in their time had to be brave.

But our first moments
with you were short.
The doctors rushed you away,
and your mother was in danger.
She badly needed care.
The choice I had to make to leave your mother's
side and follow you was terrible,
but for you, I had to be brave.

I watched the nurses work to help you
while they tried to explain to me
what was happening.
Exhausted and heartsick,
I kept telling myself:
you must be brave.

When I knew you were in good hands,
I ran through the hospital
to get back to your mother's room,
not knowing what I would find.
I thought about the wonderful memories
I had of my mother.

I remembered the powwows
she took me to when I was young.
I remembered the singing
that would fill your ears,
the drumbeat you could feel in your soul,
the dancers so full of grace in their regalia.
This was how my mother showed me who we are,
and passed to me the gift of my culture.

I wondered in fear if you would lose the chance
to have memories like these of your own.
Without your mother by my side,
I didn't know if I would be able to be brave.

My mother, your grandmother,
used to take me, my sister,
and brothers with her
to visit her brother, our uncle.
We were amazed by his collection:
spears, bows, arrows, and a shield as well.
They had been made
by indigenous people like us in the past.

My mother believed
it was important for us
to see these pieces of our heritage,
and to know how proud
our uncle was of being Native
American. My mother taught me
that to be proud of who you are
is to be brave.

When I reached the hospital room,
the doctor told me at the door that she had done her work,
and your mother was out of danger.
As I walked to her side, I knew I should be strong for her.
She struggled with her recovery and was always in pain,
but the smile never left her face.
I never knew someone could be so brave.

The sun rose, and your mother finally got to hold you.
We felt the worst had passed, that we had made it.
But just as we believed our life with you was about to start,
another storm decided to turn our way.

I put my arms around you and your mother and told myself:
be brave, be brave, be brave.

A historic storm named Hurricane Harvey
approached our hometown of Corpus Christi, Texas.
The sun was out and the wind was barely blowing,
but off in the distance the sky was darkening.
You could feel that something was coming.

Thirteen hours after your birth,
as the weather predictions became grave,
the hospital evacuated you to San Antonio
in an ambulance with your nurse.
As we followed behind in our car,
we were so sad for our family,
our home, and our neighbors,
but we knew that they would be brave.

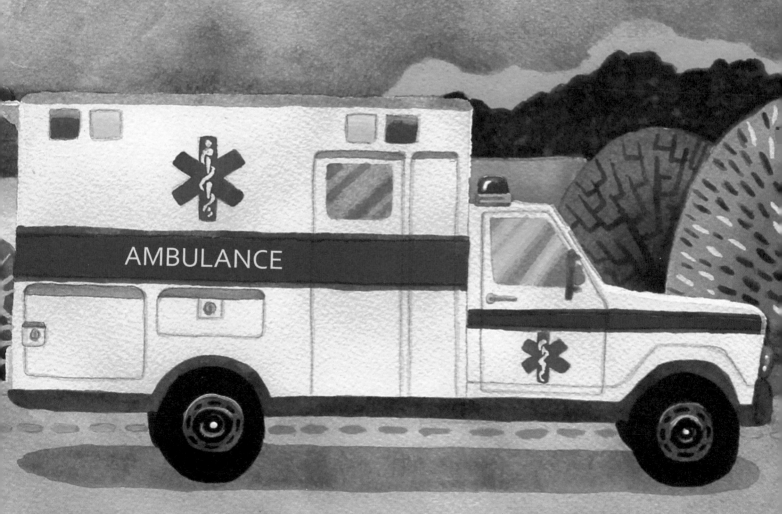

On the road to San Antonio
the traffic was backed up for miles.
All of the people were leaving behind
everything they had, uncertain of the future.
As our Native ancestors were forced to leave their homes
by strangers who claimed it for their own,
we were also on a trip we didn't want to make,
unsure if we'd be able to return.
That they found the courage and strength to endure their struggle
helped me understand what it means to be brave.

With so many fleeing the storm,
the drive to San Antonio took twice as long as normal.
It gave me time to think about
how much I wanted to share my heritage with you,
as my mother had with me, though I don't know how.
Our connection to our tribe is lost to us;
gone with a relative no one remembers or even met.
The journey to reconnect with the people and traditions
we were separated from will require much from us,
but for you Lakota, I will be brave.

EVACUATION ROUTE

When the storm passed and it was safe to return,
we saw the damage the hurricane had done.
We saw Rockport, Texas, with its houses collapsed,
boats on land, and debris piled high.
We were lucky that our home was spared the worst,
when so many South Texans had suffered terribly.

But the courage of our neighbors held strong.
I wanted to be out there with them
doing my part to help rebuild,
but after all you and your mother had been through,
I was needed at home.
Our friends delivered tank after tank of fresh water to the
towns of Port Aransas, Rockport, and Aransas Pass for days, as
the families there were without even clean water to drink.
With the support of each other,
our community showed its determination to be brave.

And then life with you started.
Your mother and I
hardly got any sleep,
but we were so happy.
One day you were crying and crying,
we couldn't figure out
what troubled you, Lakota.
But I knew who to call.

Soon your aunt arrived
with your grandmother
and great-grandmother to help.
I held you up to them in my hands.
Your great-grandmother brought out
a bundle of dried sage and lit the end on fire,
blessing you with its fragrant, gentle smoke.
In no time you were calmed,
and fell into a very peaceful sleep.
It reminded me of something
from my childhood
I'd forgotten.

When I was a little boy,
my mother would perform this same ritual every month.
She would burn sage throughout the house
to ward off the negative energy and bless our home.
Early in the morning
she would come into my room
and go to the four corners, reciting words
under her breath and interrupting my sleep.

I didn't understand then,
but I know now that this was her way
of giving us her love and protection,
just as I give you mine, little Lakota.

Watching your great-grandmother
give the same blessing to you
reminded me that you have a beautiful family
that will always be here for you,
even when you cannot be brave.

I knew a moment had arrived.
We took you to your room to put you down for bed,
gazing in amazement at the life we had created.
Your mother sat next to me while I had a talk with you.

I had thought about this moment all my life.
There were two words I wanted you to have with you always,
two words that would be there for you
when times got tough, two words to always fall back on
when you don't know what to do:

BE BRAVE

I told you folktales and legends about our Native ancestors,
how they lived, and stood up for their way of life in the past.
I told you of Geronimo who persisted, Cochise who led,
Crazy Horse who fought, Chief Joseph who resisted,
and Sitting Bull who united.

Each from different tribes, but joined by the adversity they faced.
To protect their people and their tradition,
they made very hard decisions.
Sometimes, to do the right thing, you have to be brave.

And then I told you
what my own life has taught me:
Embracing a culture and heritage whose traditions
are unknown to most of the people you meet
will call for you to be brave.

You will grow up in two worlds, with different beliefs,
and it will be difficult because not everyone will understand,
but you need to be brave.

You must be who you are.
Show everyone that you are proud to be Native American.
To say it, is to be brave.

Have a good heart, show compassion, respect people,
and for those who aren't able,
I expect you to be brave.

Your mother and I will always be here for you, Lakota,
and when you go out on your own, remember what we taught you.
Most of all, always remember to be brave.

Author's Note

Be Brave, Be Brave, Be Brave is not only about bravery; it's also about goodness—the goodness, or compassion, that compels us to help others, even when bad things happen, when we're facing the unknown, when we're scared, and when we feel alone. Even at the expense of ourselves.

There are many examples of this kind of bravery in the story, and also some that didn't make it to print. Like the nurses and doctors in the Newborn Intensive Care Unit at Bay Area Medical Center who continued to work as the winds and rain of Hurricane Harvey bore down on Corpus Christi. Lakota's nurse, Tess, traveled with him to San Antonio in the ambulance, and took care of him while he was in the NICU at Methodist Stone Oak Hospital. Evie and the NICU staff at Stone Oaks were also amazing, and we will always be grateful for the care they gave Lakota. There were other nurses who traveled with the hospital evacuees as well, leaving behind their families and loved ones. They made a choice to "be brave" for the sick children, to keep them safe from the storm. Every one of them is an inspiration in my eyes.

Searching for your Native ancestors usually starts with a family story. Mine came from my grandmother, who told me about my great-great-grandmother Victoria. She was born in the late 1800s, and according to my grandmother, was a Native American woman of the Apache tribe.

Proof of your heritage is often established by discovering an ancestor's name on the Tribal Roll. In Victoria's time, when Native Americans were forced from their lands by the US government and relocated to areas called "reservations," the Tribal Roll was a record that the people would sign their names to when they arrived at their new land.

It is unclear why my ancestors broke from their tribe, though not all Native Americans went to a reservation. Many fled to Canada and Mexico, while some chose to live their lives in the towns that were built on top of their original homes. While much was lost, many traditions and cultural practices were handed down, like the sage blessing my grandmother performed for Lakota. These stories led me to research my records on the internet, and to take a DNA test, which confirmed that I am nearly half Native American.

But my journey to find my tribe continues. I recently became friends with a Lipan Apache medicine man, who bestowed a blessing upon my family. He discovered his ancestry late in his life by using a researcher. I hope that this friendship might bring me one step closer to reconnecting with my people. It is a difficult road, but for my son, I will be brave.

Dedications

To my wife, Vicky, you make me a better person every day, all because you chose me. Thank you for dreaming with me, believing in me, and loving me. I always wonder how I got so lucky.

To my son, Lakota, you have given me a happiness I have never experienced: that of a father. You have inspired me to reach for the stars, and taught me what it means to be brave. May you always have a young soul, live a long life, and have the heart of a warrior. No matter where my writing takes me, know that you, Lakota, are my greatest creation.

–F. Anthony Falcon

There are many people who inspired and enabled me to illustrate my first children's book, and they all deserve recognition.

First, I'd like to thank my parents. They supported my decision to attend art school and fully believed that I would be able to make a living as a creator, or whatever else I chose to be in life. They never doubted or judged my decisions.

Second, many thanks to all of my professors at the Herron School of Art + Design. You laid the foundation I needed to begin building the structure of my career. Thank you for never sugarcoating your critiques, and for always being available to me as valuable resources–and more importantly, as friends.

Last, my best friend and partner in life, Jack. Without his love, care, and hard work, I never would have been able to take the time and space I needed to complete this project. Your confidence in me gives me the will to keep pursuing my dream. You are my anchor in this stormy sea of life.

–Trisha Mason

BE BRAVE, BE BRAVE, BE BRAVE

Text © 2019 by F. Anthony Falcon
Illustrations © 2019 by Trisha Mason

Published by POW! a division of
powerHouse Packaging & Supply, Inc.
32 Adams Street,
Brooklyn, NY 11201-1021
info@powkidsbooks.com
www.powkidsbooks.com
www.powerHouseBooks.com
www.powerHousePackaging.com

Printed and bound by Asia Pacific Offset

Book design by Krzysztof Poluchowicz

Library of Congress Control Number: 2018967553

ISBN: 978-1-57687-914-6

10 9 8 7 6 5 4 3 2 1

Printed in China